MY FAITH
Spiritual Baptist Christian

Teacher Hazel Ann Gibbs De Peza, Ed.D

WORKBOOK ESS LLC
187 E Warm Springs Rd,
Suite B285, Las Vegas, NV 89119, USA
Website: https://workbookpress.com/
Hotline: 1-888-818-4856
Email: admin@workbookpress.com

Ordering Information:

Quantity sales. Special discounts are available on quantity purchases by corporations, associations, and others.

For details, contact the publisher at the address above.

Library of Congress Control Number:

ISBN-13:   978-1-958176-56-6 (Paperback Version)
               978-1-958176-57-3 (Digital Version)

REV. DATE: 06/01/2022

MY FAITH:

SPIRITUAL BAPTIST CHRISTIAN

TEACHER HAZEL

REV. DR. HAZEL ANN GIBBS DE PEZA

```
        C
        H
        R
SPIRITUAL I BAPTIST
        S
        T
        I
        A
        N
```

Ye know that ye were Gentiles, carried away unto these dumb idols, even as ye were led. Wherefore I give you to understand, that no man speaking by the Spirit of God calleth Jesus accursed: and that no man can say that Jesus is the Lord, but by the Holy Ghost. Now there are diversities of gifts, but the same Spirit. And there are differences of administrations, but the same Lord. And there are diversities of operations, but it is the same God which worketh all in all.

1 Corinthians 12:2-6

****

They shall lay their hands on you, and persecute you, delivering you up to the synagogues, and into the prisons, being brought before kings and rulers for my name's sake. And it shall turn to you for a testimony. Settle it therefore in your hearts, not to meditate before what ye shall answer. For I will give you a mouth and wisdom, which all your adversaries shall not be able to gainsay or resist.

Luke 21:12-15

****

And it shall come to pass afterwards, that I will pour out my spirit upon all flesh, and your sons and your daughters shall prophesy, your old men shall dream dreams, your young men shall see visions.

Joel 2:28

****

CONTENTS

ACKNOWLEDGMENTS

My thanks go, first of all, to Almighty God, through His Son Jesus Christ by whose blood I am redeemed in the mystery working power of the Holy Spirit, Guide and Comforter.

I must acknowledge my friend, Michael Ramcharan, Executive Director of CEPACASA, who insisted that it was time for me to publish, as well as his members of staff, Judy and Claudia.

I will not forget my sister in Christ, Phyllis, who typed the first two versions of this work and forced me to become friends with the computer for this version. And of course, thank you Lystra Ann for the "apples".

I specially thank Dr. Everard Johnston, Dean of the Seminary of St. John Vianney and the Ugandan Martyrs for his insightful editing and Dr. Ival Melville Myers for graciously consenting to read and comment.

My gratitude to the stars of my life, my three sons, for staying sweet, shining, and supportive.

Thank you too, my mentor/advisor Bishop R.R. Thomas.

I pay tribute to my Faith, the Spiritual Baptist Christian Faith and all the Patriarchs who stood firm in the faith, suffered much, and sang about a day they did not live to see, but who believed in their hearts that, **His Truth Will Keep Marching On.**

PREWORD

**Howbeit, when He, the Spirit of Truth,
Is come, He will guide you into all Truth.
(John 16:13)**

This work is produced in response to a request by the Ministry of Education, arising out of my objection to the misinformation being taught through the Social Studies curriculum in the schools of the nation, and the expressed need by teachers and the national community for information on the Spiritual Baptist Faith, particularly in light of the granting of **"Spiritual Baptist/Shouter Liberation Day"** as a public holiday.

I am a Spiritual Baptist. I am a Christian. Spiritual Baptist Christians believe in Jesus Christ as King of Kings, Lord of Lords, True God and True Man, Saviour of souls, Redeemer of mankind and **The Only Mediator** between God and man.

We believe that the Holy Spirit of God is alive and working in the world today as Comforter and Guide according to the promises of Jesus Christ to His apostles. We believe in the unity and the trinity of the Godhead. We believe that God is a Spirit and they who worship Him must worship Him in spirit and in truth.

This text seeks to correct the "misconceptions perpetuated by scholars and laymen who are not yet aware that 'Spiritual Baptists are no longer perceived in the way in which European colonial society and their black collaborators wanted us to see them; as religious cranks, odd balls, and crack pots'. "Misconceptions which produce fear in the minds of the uninitiated and which are themselves the products of fear, fear of self" (Gibbs De Peza 1989).

Its material is taken largely from my two theses lodged at the University of the West Indies and the paper presented at the Conference of 1996 and reproduced in the book, *Call Him By His Name Jesus*. There are, of course, some new thoughts and insights applied to the material, but some things remain constant.

The ongoing debates about the nature of the Faith are considered in the Chapter Growth and Society, for the author seeks not to evade difficult issues or deny reality but to reveal the facts and to unmask the truth. When one knows the truth, one has free choice and is empowered by truth to make one's choice and to do so wisely.

May this text serve to dispel the myths and fallacies which abound about the Spiritual Baptist Faith and thus reduce the biases and prejudices which colour and constrain much of the interaction of the general citizenry with members of the Faith and with matters concerning the Faith. And may the teachers of our nation and indeed all readers follow the study code as elucidated by E.B. ldowu, quoted in Gibbs De Peza 1989, that:

**In the study of religion,
The FIRST RULE
in the scholar's code is
*CAUTION;***

**The SECOND RULE:
*OPENNESS;***

**The THIRD RULE:
*REVERENCE.***

The first reprint of the book in March 2007, eight years after the first publication in 1999, sought to fill the growing need for material on the Faith. For as the celebration of the national holiday, Spiritual/Shouter Baptist Liberation Day, every March 30, in Trinidad and Tobago, became more acknowledged by the national community, and the Faith more accepted by the Christian community, the greater grew the demand for authentic information on the Faith.

This republication in 2022, provides improved accessibility and electronic availability, and updates the status of the Organizational Structure and Development of the Spiritual/Shouter Baptist Faith. The Faith's history remains the same, for the facts do not change, but living organisms grow and this publication must, of necessity, be faithful to truth and provide the image of the growth (Chapter Two) and achievement (Chapter Four) relevant to and consonant with the time of republication for the Baptist community, the wider Christian community, and the world in general.

INTRODUCTION

Jesus saith unto him,
'I am the Way, the Truth, and the Life.
No man cometh unto the Father, but by Me'.
(John 14:6)

T he Spiritual Baptist Faith is the name given to the religious group emerging among Africans in the nineteenth century in Trinidad. They were called "Shouters" when, in November 1917, the **Shouter's Prohibition Ordinance, Act #27, 1917** was being passed against their mode of worship which was considered to be 'too noisy' and 'too African', and therefore uncivilized and unacceptable.

The name Spiritual/Shouter Baptist is specific to Trinidad and Tobago as Revival is to Jamaica and Shaker is to St. Vincent, and the movement parallels those movements in the named islands. The 19th Century saw the abolition of slavery and the emergence and growth of "folk religions" i.e. indigenised forms of Christianity and reinterpreted and syncretized forms of African Traditional religions, throughout the diaspora wherever Africans had been granted their freedom. Varying names were given to these movements in the various islands or areas of their birth and growth. Because of the nature of the origin and growth of the Faith, any discussion of it brings to the fore the argument whether it is an African or a Christian religious group. A rational deduction will indicate that it is both African and Christian. But this position is not easily accepted by adherents and non-adherents alike.

On the one hand, the Eurocentric Christian view is that to be Christian it cannot be African. A position arising out of the effects of Colonial stigmatization and the Prohibition on society's attitude, and based on the perception, succinctly expressed in "Traditional Enactments of Trinidad" by Rawle Gibbons.

> Society in the Caribbean is fleshed on the basic, stubborn assumption of white superiority ... it is still believed that the sons of bondage can find salvation only in whiteness; things African are still regarded as vulgar, violent, or evil. (Quoted in Gibbs De Peza 1996 (a))

On the other hand, the growth of Afro-consciousness has led to an anti-Christian view, a Euro-Christian resistance, which seeks to break the 'Christian hegemony'. This position claims, to quote one of its proponents, from a conversation on the topic that,

> Christianity with its white Jesus cannot be the religion of Africans since it denigrates the Ancestors and the African traditions.

Both positions ignore certain realities about culture, religion, civilization, and Christianity. In following the history of the Faith, therefore, the author fords the streams of Africa and Trinidad, and Christianity to arrive at the whole picture. The 'whole picture' is a complex collage. As the Faith grew and the society developed many changes took place, new pieces were added, and new streams developed which no true history can ignore. In spite of the deviations and the new dimensions, there is still a basic structure and that too is explained in detail.

CHAPTER ONE

STREAMS OF ORIGIN

(i) From Africa Land – The People

(ii) From Jordan Bank – The Faith

(I) FROM AFRICA LAND - THE PEOPLE

Blessed be Egypt my people,
and Assyria the work of my hands
and Israel mine inheritance.
(Isaiah 19:25)

' T he most southerly isles of the Caribbean archipelago' is the tourist-directed description of Trinidad and Tobago, the twin island republican nation. It is known as the land of calypso, limbo and steel-band. It is, too, the location for the emergence of the Spiritual Baptists also called Shouters.

The 'Father of the Nation', Eric Eustace Williams, in his *History of the People of Trinidad and Tobago* (1964) describes early Trinidad thus:

> After the discovery by Columbus in 1498, Trinidad remained almost completely neglected by Spain until 1538... Little was accomplished in the way of effective possession of Trinidad by Sedeno and thereafter the island lapsed into virtual oblivion ... throughout the 17th and 18th centuries Trinidad languished, a Spanish colony in name, a forgotten and underdeveloped island in fact, Governors came and went, but Trinidad continued to languish. (Williams, p. 11)

Into that 18th century situation came "Africa to the Rescue" (the title of chapter 4). In Chapter 4 of his book, Williams records the reason, origin and perpetuation of the "historical lie of African inferiority" (Williams, p. 30) and its effect on the Africans brought to the West Indies.

It is among this "different species of the same genus equal in intellectual faculties to the orangutan" (quoted by Williams, p. 31 from the writings of a Jamaican planter, Edward Long, in 1774) that the Shouter/Spiritual Baptist Faith emerged. Williams is quick to note however, that, in spite of the prevailing European perception of African inferiority, the Africans had indeed come from a continent that,

> Was in full efflorescence, in all the splendour of harmonious and well-informed civilizations, an efflorescence which the European conquistadors annihilated as far as they progressed. (Williams, p, 36)

3

So, contrary to general opinion, the Africans who came, came with a history, a consciousness and a culture.

Williams acquiesces with Herskovits that,

> The Shouters and the Shango... have come to Trinidad straight from Africa. So have the traditions of burials, especially in respect of wakes... most important of all, the calypso for which Trinidad has become famous... is in the African Tradition ... These were the people who came in their thousands to the West Indies, though in relatively limited numbers to Trinidad during the slave period, to develop ... 'a magnificent superstructure of American commerce on an African foundation'. (Williams, p. 39)

Thus it is that, in 18th century Trinidad, he suggests, Spain set out to:

> Transform a backward Amerindian colony governed by Spain into a Spanish colony run by Frenchmen and worked by African slaves. (Williams, p. 40)

In 1783, the Spanish cedula of population saw Africans brought from the other Caribbean islands to Trinidad. By 1797, the British ruled the island and another source of Africans became the African soldiers who had fought on the British side during the War of American Independence (1776 - 1783). They arrived in 1803. Again between 1813 and 1816 companies of African soldiers, ex-slaves were settled in Trinidad. In the histories written about the Company Villages and the Baptist Missionary Society in Trinidad, these African soldiers, ex-slaves, described as Merikins, African Americans, are reported to have brought the Baptist Faith with them.

It was obvious, therefore, that many Africans came or were brought to Trinidad and the pattern was that the colony simply absorbed within its boundaries divers and diverse groups of African peoples.

When these large masses of Africans were being dislocated:

> No one sought to find out what religions they practised. Religious denomination was neither barrier nor criterion for enslavement. By that time Africa was well-acquainted with Islam and Christianity in addition to the many groupings of the African Traditional Religion. Moreover, the Africans who were landed here had not been given a direct trip from their homeland. They had sojourned at other ports and/or been seasoned for the task and tarrying here. (Gibbs De Peza 1996 (b))

> Then slavery was abolished and the Africans were free. Because religion is an integral part of life for the African, they began to practise the religions they had come with. Christianity was definitely among them. The Orisha religion of Nigeria was not the only religion with which the Africans came. They practiced the religions they knew. (Gibbs De Peza 1996 (b))

Not all of the Africans who came were Christians neither did they all choose to follow Christianity. Of those who chose Christianity some settled for the prevailing denominations of the status quo and became Anglicans, Catholics, Presbyterians, or Methodists, and some chose to be Baptists. Some chose to be officially one thing and secretly another. Others chose to uphold the traditional religions of the homeland.

Bishop Eudora Thomas in her work *Short History of the Spiritual Baptist (commonly called 'Shouters')* acknowledges that:

> The history and origin of the Spiritual Baptist Faith in Trinidad and Tobago are somewhat vague and have not been studied in detail. Relatively little is known about the first Spiritual Baptist Leader. The location of the first Spiritual Baptist Church in Trinidad and Tobago has not been identified. (Thomas p. 1)

But with other writers who sought to document their knowledge of the Faith she agrees,

> That the Faith slowly developed sometime during the nineteenth century ... The Faith can be considered about the only indigenous religious group in Trinidad and Tobago... the Spiritual Baptists or Shouters played a large role in spreading the knowledge of Christianity throughout the islands, by their evangelical labours, crusades, byways and hedges preaching to all who cared to listen. Their duty was to make the teachings of Jesus Christ known. (Thomas, p. 1)

Growing alongside the Spiritual Baptist/Shouters was the African Traditional Religion (Shango). Because the adherents of both religions were of the same kith and kin many similarities abounded, similarities in cultural practices, in world view and in attitudes. As a result of the similarities and of an absence of documentation and teaching of the practices of the two religions, some syncretization took place and a fusion and confusion arose in the minds of members and non-members alike.

Of the Africans who chose to uphold the traditional African religions, some followed the Orisha tradition, the local reinterpretation of the Yoruba beliefs, often referred to as Shango. It must be noted that **Orisha does not claim the death of Christ as atonement for sin** and still practises blood sacrifice as did the followers of Judaism, in the Old Testament. (Many Jews followed Christ but many held on to their old religion).

Orisha devotees are possessed by powers other than the Holy Spirit. For Spiritual Baptists "spirit-possession" is in the form of the manifestation of the indwelling of the Holy Spirit. **Orisha (Shango) and Spiritual Baptists are two distinct belief systems, separate and apart.** The one (Orisha) believes in the need for sacrifice, the other (Spiritual Baptist) believes that the crucifixion of Jesus Christ is the last and final sacrifice, for therein is man justified. At the cross, man's redemption was paid in full.

Because both religions have icons of Africa and are characterized by rhythmic singing and movements in their services some people erroneously claim that they are the same or that one came from the other. The fact is that they both developed out of the same cultural situation during the same period of time. One is not the forerunner of the other. One did not give birth to the other.

The Spiritual Baptist Faith developed among those Africans who chose to maintain the spontaneity of their Africanness; who have fused their African background with the tenets of Christianity to produce a religion which is the result of enculturation and is therefore more like a part of life, and more exciting. The Spiritual Baptist Faith can justly be described as:

> the attempt of the Negro to establish bench marks for freedom ... to fashion out of the religious elements in the community, something more fitting to the needs of the people, a worship more realistic. (quoted in Gibbs De Peza 1989)

Indeed, **the Spiritual Baptists were affirming Christ as the head of their Faith and their Africanness as integral to that affirmation.** On November 28, 1917, the Shouter Prohibition Ordinance was passed in the colony of Trinidad making illegal the activities of the Shouters. In leading the debate on the issue on November 16, 1917, the then Attorney General claimed, inter alia that:

> The Shouters have had a somewhat stormy history ... they seem ... to have flourished exceedingly in St. Vincent, and to have made themselves such an unmitigated nuisance that they had to be legislated out of existence. They then came to Trinidad and continued complaints have been received by the Government. (Hansard, quoted in Jacobs, p. 96)

Thus, even the Legislative Council found no difficulty in erroneously labeling the origin of the Faith as of St. Vincent and in following the pattern set in St. Vincent in 1912 outlawing the Spiritual Baptists/Shouters. This was the religion of the ex-slave community of whom the English novelist Trollope said,

> he has made no approach to the civilization of his white fellow creatures, whom he imitates as a monkey does a man. (quoted in Williams, p. 31)

In 1996, in his **"Declaration Of The Spiritual Baptist/ Shouter Holiday"**, the Prime Minister of Trinidad and Tobago stated that,

> The Shouters, the practitioners of the Spiritual Baptist Faith was formed sometime prior to 1917. It was a new religion in the Colony at the time and because of the manner in which the men and women practised their faith, numerous complaints reached the Government about "disturbance of the peace" by inter alia, shouting, ringing of bells and chanting by the "Shouters". (Declaration, p. 2)

Indeed, one is inclined to consider a thought provoking position adopted by Michael Ramcharan,

> One must wonder that at the height of the First World War the legislature in Trinidad would be discussing the noise a group of people made while practising their religion. I

believe that there was more to it.

The Shouters Prohibition Ordinance of 1917 was a direct attempt by the plantocracy and the Colonial Authorities to destroy this effort of the ex-slaves at unity. The beatings, imprisonment and fines resulting from infractions of the Ordinance bear witness to the tenacity of our people in the face of difficulty. (Ramcharan in Gibbs De Peza 1996 (b))

There is no official documentation of the early beginnings of the Spiritual Baptist Faith. But the available histories of Trinidad and the works written about religion in Trinidad as well as the few writings on the Spiritual Baptist Faith and the oral tradition, both within the Baptist community and among the general citizenry, provide sufficient proof that the people among whom the Spiritual Baptist Faith emerged were the Africans of the slave and ex-slave community residing in Trinidad. That the Spiritual Baptist Faith was not brought here in the early 20th century is further supported by the records of the arrival of George Cowen in 1843 after emancipation and before 1912 and 1917. For it is recorded that in Cowen's attempts to assist by offering the administration and respectability of the Baptist Missionary Society of London to the existing Baptist community he insisted that "worshippers under cover of the BMS were required to give up shouting and the manifestation of spirit possession." (quoted in Gibbs De Peza 1989).

In the Foreword to J.M. Hackshaw's *The Baptist Denomination (1992)*, Rev. A.J. Parkes lamented, "one can clearly understand that, unlike many missionary fields of endeavour where the missionary societies pioneered and established work in accordance with their orthodox practice, the Baptist Missionary Society of England had to accommodate practices and beliefs that had been established for twenty-seven years by the original pioneers of the Faith before B.M.S. arrival." (Hackshaw, p. ii)

Thus, the efforts of the Baptist Missionary Society under George Cowen to enforce orthodoxy on the Baptists, whom he met already practising their faith, occasioned a split among the Baptist fraternity so that:

> By the end of the century (1800's) three distinct groups had emerged .... "The London Baptists" .... "Independents" ... and
> another group ... first known as "Wayside" and "Candle" Baptists, but today, as "Spiritual Baptists". (Hackshaw, pp. 19-20)

1. *The London Baptist (Company Baptist)* – those Churches which accepted the 'Charter of Affiliation from the Baptist Missionary Society of London' who are characterized by orthodoxy and supervision from outside. The English missionary provided instructions in the way of conducting services and other church matters.

2. *The Independent Baptist (The Disobedient Baptist)* – those churches which withdrew from foreign supervision, refused to integrate with the Baptist Missionary Society and preferred to control

their own affairs. They paralleled the London Baptist in that they also gave up 'shouting' and the manifestation of spirit possession but maintained an entirely local leadership and folk character in recruiting new leaders. In 1966 they were finally incorporated as The Independent Baptist Mission Churches of Trinidad and Tobago.

3.   *The Wayside/Candle/Shouter/Spiritual Baptist* – the third group, those who remained, who did not join the BMS, who walked the byways and highways preaching the Gospel, calling man to repentance after the manner of John the Baptist and Jesus the Christ and whose worship is characterized by 'shouting, catching the power and mourning'.

The Spiritual Baptist journey which began with the uprooting from Africa has not ended. From 1917 onwards through the 1951 Repeal of the Prohibition Ordinance the journey has been long and painful.

The punishment meted out to people of the Faith became symbols of the struggle by Spiritual Baptists to hold on to their beliefs. Practising their religion clandestinely brought many consequences but positively it ensured the continuity of the Faith. (Ramcharan in Gibbs De Peza 1996 (b))

(II) FROM JORDAN BANK - THE FAITH

Then, cometh Jesus from Galilee
to Jordan unto John,
to be baptized of him.
(Matthew 3:13)

It is generally acknowledged by the various sects of 'Baptistdom' throughout the world where Baptist churches are functioning, and so it is also for the Spiritual Baptists of Trinidad and Tobago, that *the Call of the Baptist Faith* commenced with the advent of John the Baptist with his cry:

"Repent Ye: for the Kingdom of Heaven is at hand." **(Matthew 3:2)**

The Initiation of the Faith occurred when Jesus was baptized by John in the River Jordan and the Holy Spirit descended in the form of a dove as recorded in ***Mark 1: 9-10.***

The Practice of the Faith originated in the great commission given to the eleven apostles by Jesus Christ before His ascension into heaven when He said unto them:

> "Go Ye therefore, and teach all nations, baptizing them in the name of the Father, and of the Son and of the Holy Ghost, teaching them to observe all things, whatsoever I have commanded you, and Lo, I am with you always even unto the end of the world." **(Matthew 28: 19-20)**

The Sanction and Sanctification of the Faith materialized on the day of Pentecost when the Holy Spirit descended in the form of cloven tongues of fire as reported in **Acts 2:1-4.**

So, the Apostles began the **'Apostolic Tradition'** and imparted their teachings from Jesus Christ to the early Christians who practised the faith of the Apostles and handed down their teachings. The Book of **'The Acts of the Apostles'** records the early history of the Apostolic Church and traces the growth of Christianity in Palestine and its spread out into Syria, Asia, Greece and Rome according to the journeys of Paul. Also recorded in **The Acts** in Chapter Eight (8) is the instruction and baptism of:

> "a man of Ethiopia, an eunuch of great authority under Candace Queen of the Ethiopians, who had the charge of all her treasure, and had come

to Jerusalem for to worship." **(Acts 8:27)**

Those adherents to the precepts of the New Testament for the church established by Christ, maintaining the apostolic tradition, practising the baptism of believers and relying on the guidance of the Holy Spirit are the ancestry of the Baptist Faith. It must be noted that there were no churches called Baptist Churches in the early centuries, but all Christians were then Baptists, in whatever part of the world they may have been found.

Early in the fourth century, the shift from believers' baptism to infant baptism was added to the errors creeping into the Church and the persecution of those who adhered to the Apostolic Doctrine heightened. Down through the centuries, before, during, and after the Reformation, these Baptists and Anabaptists continued to suffer and die for the true faith of Jesus Christ.

A local Independent Baptist Minister Rev. Fitzroy Richardson in T*he Origin of the Baptists* notes, about the Baptist Faith, as do many eminent religious historians that:

> the Baptists date their unbroken history back
> to the time when God called John the Baptist
> to prepare the way for the introduction of the
> Christ to a lost and benighted world.
> (Richardson, p. 5)

The oral tradition of the nation indicates that early in the 19th century members of the Shouter/Spiritual Baptist Faith walked the streets of villages and towns calling men to repentance and issuing warnings of destruction to come. For this they were also called Wayside Baptists. It is reported that the Shouters or Wayside Baptists amidst the 'noise' and 'disturbances' of their practice were preaching repentance and Baptism according to the Holy Bible for the remission of sins.

"The Shouter Baptists then claimed that the Bible is the basis of their religion and that all their practices could be traced to the Bible" (Jacobs p. 287). It is recorded in the first case tried after the passing of the Bill in 1917 that the defendants and witnesses walked with their Bibles and referred to its contents in support of their services. So strong was their faith that one leader is recorded to have said "as Nebuchadnezzar throw de three Hebrew children in de fiery furnace, I make up me mind to turn a jail bud for Jesus Christ." (quoted in Jacobs, p. 142)

Viola Gopaul Whittington who, in her *History and Writings of the Spiritual Baptist Faith* sets out to "show that the Spiritual Baptist is an off-shoot from the Orisha Cult which came through invocation" (Gopaul Whittington, Intro. p. vii) after some deliberation on various aspects of slave life and slave belief contradicts her intention and acknowledges and explains:

> Under Christ a new dispensation was unfurled, for under him all things were made new ... The New Testament is interpreted in every phase of the Spiritual Baptist Faith, as they stand on the principles laid down by Christ the way-shower, the self-same Christ whom, as the Son of God the Bible credited him to be (sic) They had been following Him since the Faith emerged. (Gopaul Whittington, pp. 7-8)

In all the reports of the Patriarchs of the Faith handed down via oral tradition there is no doubt or question that the first 'Shouters' or Spiritual Baptists were Christians, 'Old Time religion' Christians in a new setting.

The various writings on the Spiritual Baptist used as references in this work all support this oral tradition. Research published by foreign scholars all acknowledge the "Christian Element" in what is generally referred to as "folk religion".

It is to be noted that the Christianity that was brought to the West Indies by the missionaries in the form of various religious denominations was no longer identical to the religious movement begun by its founder, Jesus Christ. The history of Christianity reveals that fundamental changes had taken place giving rise to the various groupings and denominations. The Reformation begun in 1517, is acknowledged as an attempt to reform the Church or return her to the early structure of Christianity.

It is to be noted further that Christianity came into existence as a new religious movement within Judaism and bore marks of enculturation into the culture of the Jews. In fact, Christianity is so indigenized to suit the various cultures among which it grew and grows that:

> The **Romans** fashioned Christianity to their culture and gave a plethora of saints, the Latin language and much pomp and ceremony in the services of Roman Catholicism; the **English** fashioned Christianity

to their culture and gave the austerity of High Church Service and the conservatism of the English in both style and language in Anglicanism; we, the **Africans**, have fashioned Christianity to our culture and given the rhythm of the drums and hand clapping, the lively sounding of trumpets, the movement of the body to match the movement of the Spirit and the rhythm and the all-embracing approach to religion as a way of life in the Alladura in Africa, the Shakers in St. Vincent, the Southern Baptists in the U.S.A. and the Spiritual Baptists here in Trinidad and Tobago. (Gibbs De Peza 1996 (b))

CHAPTER TWO

GROWTH AND SOCIETY

***O, let the nations be glad and
sing for joy; for thou shalt...
govern the nations upon earth.
(Ps. 67:4)***

We have seen, in Chapter One, the cultural millieu of Trinidad in the 18th and 19th centuries when the Africans came or were brought here, as well as the attitudes of the plantocracy to the peasantry or slave population. When emancipation of the slaves came, alongside it came new issues, viz ... **employment, residence, family structure, education and religion.**

Before emancipation, the responsibility for these issues lay with the slave owners. They were the employers, so they determined what work one did; they provided living quarters; they ensured that there was no family structure by separating offsprings from progenitors and allowing no husband-wife relationships to develop; they made the decisions in the domain of education since they determined who was apprenticed to which trade. Religion i.e. Christianity, was an icon of civilization and therefore unnecessary and "non- existent" for the slaves.

> In the British system religion was for the masters, not for the slaves. All religious practices on the part of the slaves were suspect and the practice of African religious custom was vigilantly suppressed. (Barrett p. 81)

History records that the Christianizing of the slaves met with strong resistance from the slave owners and when accepted and permitted it was a 'devious piety' as shown in The edict of the Bishop of London in 1727 to the slave owners in America, Sec. II where it is noted that:

> their (slaves) being baptized and becoming Christians makes no manner of change in it (their out-ward condition) ... Christianity takes not out of the hands of Superiors any degrees of strictness and severity that fairly appears to be necessary for the preserving subjection and government. (C.C. Jones, *Religious Instruction of the Negroes in the U.S. 1842* quoted in Barrett pp. 46, 47)

The ex-slaves were now faced with responsibilities and choices for which they were neither ready nor equipped. But the days came and went and life had to go on. While employment and education proved elusive, residence was taken up wherever it was found, and family structures and religion developed according to circumstances and memory, both collective and individual.

The African ethic acknowledges "the religious nature of the cosmos making no distinction between the sacred and the secular" (Mulrain, quoted in Gibbs De Peza 1989). The Africans, therefore, began practicing the religions which they knew as best as they could then recall, for in the **"experience** of religion, there is something universal and permanent" (Idowu quoted in Gibbs De Peza 1989). It is the **"expression"** of religion that is dependent on circumstance and condition: local, physical, mental, and social.

The expression of the Spiritual Baptist Faith that grew out of this new and new world situation, tempered by cultural contact and a traditional religious ethos, displays those elements present in every living religion, **changelessness and change**. The **changelessness** of the belief in One True Living Creator God, who has the whole world in his hands remains at the centre of the belief system, alongside the knowledge that "there is a force or power of energy in the universe, which can be tapped by those who know how to do so." (Mbiti quoted in Gibbs De Peza 1989)

The **change** resides in the approach to this Almighty God and the methods of acknowledging the expression of His love for us and our reverence for Him.

The Spiritual Baptist Faith, therefore, evolved slowly over time, as people responded to the situations of their life and as they chose to reflect upon their various experiences. The **experience** provided Christianity in the forms of Catholic and Protestant denominations by the Whites and the Baptist denomination by the Blacks. It was mainly because of the non-conformist sects and "their doctrine of liberty under God for the slaves, that many slaves were brought in the Christian religion" (Barrett p. 49). It also provided the African Traditional Religions in the forms of Orisha, Rada and Congo, and Islam.

The **millieu** consisted of the Christianizing of Africans by missionaries and the acceptance and/or non-acceptance of same; the retaining of the African tradition, or the denouncing of it, or even the denial of its existence; the ostensible practice of one religion and secret belief in another; the masking of African Traditional Beliefs by Catholic practices and the practice of both Christianity and African Traditional Beliefs side by side.

Some accepted the Christianity of the status quo and became faithful Anglicans, Catholics et al. Some rejected Christianity and kept the Faith of their Ancestors in Yoruba and Rada communities. Some masked the African tradition by parallel Christian practices, for example, calling the deities by saint names. Some went to Mass in the Catholic Church first, then engaged in their traditions after, "using one spiritual resource to supplement and complement the other." (Warner-Lewis, p. 51)

Still, some "Africanised their new Faith with new ring, shouts and spirituals" (Young, p.8). They accepted the tenets of Christianity, the Christian experience, and indigenized the expression of Christianity to produce the **Spiritual Baptist Faith, an indigenous Faith which has evolved in response to life situations** as has Christianity throughout its history.

Indeed, Christianity rests on a continuum of cultural expressions fashioned by the locations and origins of the people who claim discipleship to Christ: Judeo-Christianity with its Mezuzah and prayer shawl, Ethiopian Orthodox Christianity traditionally accepted to have been established by Matthew and Bartholomew of the Bible, with rigorous fasting and Sabbath keeping, Roman Christianity with an infallible Pope as its Head and a celibate clergy, Anglo-Christianity with an English Royal Sovereign as its Head and married clergy, and among the many groups of Protestant Christianity, Baptists with baptism by immersion for believers only, and a congregational form of government, all representative of its early history of enculturation.

> Since we have no problem accepting Roman Catholicism as Christianity and no one attempts to define it as Ancient Roman religion mixed with Christianity, nor with accepting Anglicanism as Christianity and no one identifies it as Ancient British or Saxon religion combined with Christianity, why then do we have a problem accepting the Spiritual Baptist Faith as Christianity and keep trying to define it as African religion mixed with Christianity? (Gibbs De Peza, 1996 (b))

The answer to that question was provided in the **Introduction**, viz. the effects of colonial stigmatization and the Prohibition on the society's attitude to things African.

Within the developing society of Trinidad was developing a living religion, Christianity in the Apostolic/ Baptist mode whose growth paralleled the growth of early

Christianity. Cottage meetings had to give way to secret meetings. Secrecy and seclusion became the order of the day. Congregations had to be kept small and manageable, an autonomous entity. In the absence of an administrative structure and formal linkages, as with the early church, changes began to develop among the various units.

We have already noted the simultaneous growth of other religions in the same setting. Fusion, syncretization, and substitution began occurring as a result of an absence of communication, documentation and teaching. With the **Repeal of the Prohibition Order in 1951** and the growing visibility of the churches and the movement, it became obvious that many churches operating under the name Spiritual/Shouter Baptist were not in fact following the Apostolic/Baptist Tradition.

It must be noted that all of these churches suffered the same indignities. Therefore, the local history is the same and "Liberation" by the Repeal of the Ordinance is meaningful to all the various strains of the religion that emerged.

With education and its resultant upward social mobility becoming more attainable to Blacks, the Faith began to have leaders and members who were not only literate but also educated. This brought to the fore questions about doctrine and practices and the need to institute **definitions and distinctions.**

One such exercise took place:

In August 1992, from the 27th to the 31st a **National Conference on the Shouter Faith** was held, organized by the St. Ann's Astar Circle of

Divine Light Ltd. At the Conference the chief celebrant stated categorically on the theme, "Towards Affirming the Shouter Faith −A Search For Identity and Integrity," *that Shouters do not believe in Jesus Christ as Lord, that the story of Jesus is a reproduction of the story of Isis and Osiris of Egyptian mythology, stolen and adapted; that the King James version of the Bible is a lie, being a false representation of the true Bible stolen from Africa by the Romans in order to force Christianity on black people ...* That Archbishop (who claimed leadership of the Orisha community to act as an opposition senator and reverted to being a Shouter Baptist Archbishop at the end of his senatorship) was, in his deliberation, expressing the view of many of like mind, that Spiritual Baptists "sold out" to the European Christianity and that Shouter Baptists do not accept the "white man's religion". (Gibbs De Peza, 1996 (b))

Responses to this Conference led to an awakening of the public and the membership to the reality that "not all in Israel are Israelites".

Another exercise in *definitions and distinctions* took place in March 1996 when the **Spiritual Baptist Conference of Delegates** took place at the Auditorium of the Eric Williams Financial complex, the Twin Towers, with the theme **"Spiritual Baptists: Christians Moving into the 21st Century".** At that Conference, Spiritual Baptists affirmed their Faith as part of the Christian Fraternity drawing parallels with their growth and beliefs to those of the early Christian Church,

Jesus Christ is the founder of the Christian Faith; the Apostles were martyred for their Faith; the harder the persecution the more the Faith spread. With the growth and the increase came errors in the Church. Paul's letters in the Epistles of the New Testament abound with the errors that began creeping into the Church. (Gibbs De Peza 1996 (b)).

Let it be remembered that changes ... were not made in a day, nor even within a year. They came about slowly and never within all Churches. Some of the churches vigorously repudiated them. So much so that in A.D. 251, the loyal churches declared non-fellowship for those churches which accepted and practised the errors. And thus, came about the first separation among the churches.

The loyal churches suffered further persecution and became known by names other than Christian, such as Montanists, Anabaptists and Baptists. Throughout the ages they held to the features of the early Church, the most noticeable *among them being democratic form of government; believer's baptism; religious liberty and the separation of church and state.* (Caroll pp. 13-14)

In like manner the Spiritual Baptist Faith emerged as an enculturated expression of Christianity among the Africans in Trinidad and Tobago and suffered persecution and changes. Thus, today, in the Spiritual Baptist Community in Trinidad and Tobago the reality is that there exists a continuum:

> consisting of the traditional Spiritual Baptist, born out of that early situation, at the centre of the continuum. On the one end are those churches with retentions from the Baptist tradition syncretized with European/ American religious practices. On the other extremity are those churches with retentions from the Baptist tradition syncretized with the African Traditional Religion. (Gibbs De Peza, 1989)

There are therefore **Spiritual Baptist Churches** managed by Spiritual Baptist leaders who have decided to disassociate themselves from the NAME Spiritual Baptist and use other names for example, Divine Army of Christ and names from the Bible, and/or discontinue the use of the vessels and bell and/or stop the practice of mourning in an attempt to become more like the established Christian churches (e.g. Anglican) in administration and appearance. They still keep their association with the membership of the Spiritual Baptist Churches, and both visit them and invite them to participate in their services and activities.

On the other side of the continuum, there are Spiritual Baptist Churches who have adopted and adapted practices which are African or Asian in origin and not supported by the New Testament. They still, however, claim Christianity and believe that Jesus is Lord.

Then there are those who have incorporated distinct Orisha and Hindu practices into their worship. They explain the Spiritual Baptist Faith as an amalgam of all religions. They acknowledge Christianity and every other religion as well. Some of these, call themselves Shouters; others, still call themselves Spiritual Baptists; yet others, Shango Baptists.

There are those who practise the Christian tradition ostensibly and alongside it they practise the Orisha tradition. They move from one dimension to the other as the need or desire arises. Some of them do not openly align themselves with the Orisha because of the stigma still attached thereto. Others openly acknowledge that they work within both traditions. *(This dichotomy is a theological impossibility since the one sacrifice obviates the other and the belief systems nullify one another).*

The names in general use fall into three categories and identify three paths of adherence to religion. They are:

Spiritual Baptists – Christians, born again believers in Jesus Christ who have relinquished the African Traditional Religion's beliefs and practices, but do not deny their Africanness. All of their practices are supported by New Testament doctrine.

Shouter Baptists – Some Shouter Baptists are identical to the Spiritual Baptists except for the difference in the name e.g. Mt. Garazin Shouter and Baptist Church Ltd. Some have blended two traditions and adopted and adapted practices and beliefs masking one with the other. Of these, some still wish to be identified with Christianity while others have no desire to be called Christians and identify their Faith as an amalgam of many religions and religious practices.

Shango Baptists (a contradiction in terms) – those whose beliefs and practices openly incorporate two traditions and who, on occasion, identify with the Spiritual

Baptists and conduct Christian services; and at other times identify with the Orisha and practise the rituals of the Orisha Tradition.

Because of the confusion of names and practices members of the first group now call themselves "Spiritual Baptist Christians" for a clearer distinction. This use of the name Christian does not meet the approval of those who fall into the other two groupings along that end of the continuum viz., Shouter Baptist and Shango Baptist. They do not wish to be so distinguished and are content to perpetuate the confusion of perception of who Spiritual Baptists are and what they believe.

Other indicators of growth in the Spiritual Baptist community are:

(i) the construction of large, elegant church buildings.

(ii) the acquisition of lands and buildings.

(iii) the establishment of Theological Schools - the **Herman Parris Spiritual Baptist Southland School of Theology** situated at La Brea, being a landmark of achievement in both physical structure and educational prowess.

(iv) the publication of Spiritual Baptist Literature by Spiritual Baptist authors.

(v) the establishment of an education fund and the granting of scholarships to Spiritual Baptist students by the **Foundation for the Academic Advancement of Spiritual Baptist Youth.**

(vi) Spiritual Baptist women are allowed to wear their 'head-ties' when being photographed for their National Identification Cards, Driver's Permits and Passports. This is also allowed and accepted at official government ceremonies and corporate functions, as well as non-Baptist religious occasions, and more significantly, at their places of employment.

(vii) Churches, dioceses and Baptist organizations, religious, educational, cultural and commercial, continue to grow and glow on the national landscape.

(viii) Educational excellence is being demonstrated among our youth who are earning scholarships, awards, and honours in several fields of endeavour and at every level of the education system both nationally and internationally.

(ix) Several Spiritual Baptist Early Childhood Care and Education Centres have been established and registered across the country along with one government assisted primary school.

(x) Increased visibility is being achieved by the growing number of Spiritual Baptist radio, and television programmes, and features, and greater recognition is given to the celebration of the national holiday, **Spiritual Baptist Shouter Liberation Day,** and Leaders of the Faith are invited to participate in national and international forums, to represent their faith community in their religious attire.

(xi) The successful implementation of twelve months of meaningful activities commemorated and celebrated the *Centenary Year of the passing of the Prohibition Ordinance of 1917* that outlawed the Faith but did not outlive the Faith and its rapidly growing community.

(xii) Assisted by the government of the day, the construction of a National Spiritual Baptist Cathedral has commenced on state lands gifted to the Spiritual Baptist community.

These achievements attest to the development of the Faith, with and within the development of the nation of Trinidad and Tobago. While at this time, a significant percentage of the society has not yet fully accepted the Spiritual Baptist as integral to the fabric of the twin island nation, meaningful progress has been made by the Faith in the society.

Launch of Centenary Commemoration Year 2017

CHAPTER THREE

THE NAME –
SPIRITUAL BAPTIST
FAITH

God is a Spirit and they that worship Him
Must worship Him in Spirit and in Truth.
(John 4:24)

S piritual denotes the belief in the active involvement of the Holy Spirit in the lives of believers in general and in the worship service in particular. Spiritual Baptists are defined by their distinctive belief in:

a) **The guidance of the Holy Spirit** – "The Holy Ghost, whom the Father will send in my name, he shall teach you all things;" **(Jn. 14: 26)** and

b) **The indwelling of the Holy Spirit** – "And on my servants and on my handmaidens I will pour out in those days of my spirit," **(Acts 2: 17-18)** manifested by spirit communication through dreams and visions, through spirit travel while praying and meditating and through the rhythmic movement of the body and speaking in tongues. **This reliance on the Holy Spirit, His work and His gifts distinguishes the Spiritual Baptists from other Christians and other Baptists.**

BAPTIST is a denomination of Christians so named because they insisted that baptism by immersion is the only true baptism. They demonstrated their views regarding the ordinance by administering it to adults only because they insisted that infants cannot fulfill the conditions of repentance and belief. Spiritual Baptists are members of the Baptist denomination whose dependence on the Spirit and manifestation of the Spirit are central to their faith.

Baptists have, over the centuries, been subdivided into groups based on differences in their views on doctrinal points other than baptism, thus there are, for example, **Fundamentalists** and **Modernists**. Here in Trinidad and Tobago subdivisions were based on affiliation or non-affiliation to the Baptist Missionary Society. (Circa 1843) Thus we have the **London Baptists** and the **Independent Baptists**; and based on the expression of the indwelling of the Holy Spirit – **Spiritual Baptists.**

FAITH indicates the belief that the religion was born, not out of the rational decision of one man or a group of men, nor as a unit of an established denomination nor a seceder from such a unit, but out of the continuation of the tradition which originated at the birth of the Christian movement on the bank of Jordan with the baptism of its author Jesus the Christ and which was practised by his Apostles and the early Christians.

The other name by which this indigenous religious movement is known here in its homeland is "Shouters". In its original and earlier use, the name Shouters was synonymous with Spiritual Baptist. The Spiritual Baptist Faith was and is often referred to as the 'Shouters' based on their mode of worship, that is the "noisy" practice of hand clapping and bell ringing, the loud mannered singing and praying and the rhythmic movements as the method of rejoicing before the Lord.

The name Spiritual/Shouter Baptist in churches and organizations wherever they are found throughout the world is indicative of the presence of citizens of Trinidad and Tobago who have transported their indigenous mode of worship and have spread and shared the Good News. In fact, many Spiritual/Shouter Baptist citizens of Trinidad and Tobago having migrated to cities throughout the world have 'started' churches in their new 'homes'.

CHAPTER FOUR

ORGANIZATIONAL STRUCTURE AND DEVELOPMENT OF THE SPIRITUAL BAPTIST CHURCH

Behold, how good and how pleasant it is
for brethren to dwell together in unity.
(Psalm 133:1)

In the Spiritual Baptist Church, there was no organizational affiliation or structure, and the Faith grew with the blossoming of individual churches, 'camps' as they were called, established as and when the Spirit gave guidance and instructions. Church membership was congregational and the control of the affairs of the church resided in each individual church with the Leader or Mother, very much in keeping with the early mode of the Baptist Denomination and the Early Christian Church.

The Leader/Pastor and Mother still maintain authority, followed by the offices of Teacher, Shepherd, Shepherdess, Prover, Watchman, Nurse, Captain, Surveyor and Healer. Many of the churches now have elected officers and committees to oversee the many functions, helps and government. Those churches that belong to a diocese also have ordained ministers who carry titles such as Deacon/ Deaconess, Reverend, Evangelist, Archdeacon, Bishop, Abbess, Mother Superior and Archbishop. Ordained offices are held in conjunction with or in addition to the Spiritual offices listed above. The Spiritual Baptist Faith can be defined as the purest democracy, spiritual democracy, for the activities of the church are guided by the movement of the Holy Spirit and administered by any member so directed. The members freely contribute to and actively participate in the worship. This active involvement of the congregation subscribes to the scriptural doctrine espoused in the second Chapter of 1 Peter, "the priesthood of all believers".

The Spiritual Baptist Faith spread among the 'belaboured and down-trodden second class citizens of the past' to which group Africans, Slaves and Free were relegated. This led to it being described by researchers and scholars as a haven or avenue of escape for "deprived, underprivileged people seeking relief from frustration." They obviously ignored two important considerations.

1. The role of religion for man, and

2. The situation existing when the religion began developing

The Founding Fathers or early Leaders and Mothers were illiterate because for the most part black people in their day were not taught to read and write.

In those not too distant days, officialdom reading the political potential of this, movement, and probably pressured by the more accepted denominations, decided to suppress the Spiritual Baptist Movement, thus sending them underground. And so in its formative years, prayer meetings of the early followers of the Faith were always secret and kept in the woods at night.

There were no churches as we have them today. Spiritual Baptist Churches took the form of thatched huts or shacks with wooden altars and benches in the remotest parts of the country. As a result, there are no Parish churches and it is not uncommon for eight or nine separate Spiritual Baptist Churches to exist in one area.

In spite of the persecution and prosecution resulting from the "ordinance to render illegal the practices of the Body known as the **'Shouters'"** and the order of the day which was **"Beat and Arrest, Fines and Imprisonment for the Spiritual Baptist"** and perhaps because of it, the Faith, like the early Christian Faith, grew and spread.

It is during those years of active and persistent harassment that the first organization of Spiritual Baptists was formulated, initiated upon a vision received by one of its leaders while he was serving a prison sentence for being a Baptist.

Several attempts to have the Government repeal the Ordinance having failed and some clauses of the Ordinance being derogatory, demeaning, and untrue, the idea to circumvent the law was promoted among a group of Elders who had come together. They sought the air of respectability by not using the name 'Shouter', which had been imposed upon them and using instead the name Spiritual

Baptist which was an indication of their identity.

T*he West Indian United Spiritual Baptist Sacred Order was established on JUNE 3, 1942, and registered as an organization by registration no. 2440 of 1942.*

It was later incorporated by an *Act of Parliament (Act 24 of 1949)* in the year 1949 under the leadership of Pastor Leo Sandiford. It was not until March 1951 that the Legislative Council met to repeal the Ordinance of 1917 after debating the Bill which sought the repeal out of a petition made by a group of "Officers of the Spiritual Baptist Faith led by Deacon Elton George Griffith". (Note the use of the name Spiritual Baptist even for an organization which specially identified itself as the representative of the "body called Shouters".)

After the repeal of the Ordinance many churches were built and rebuilt, services were kept openly and several other Spiritual Baptist Organizations were registered as they sought to unite in order to regularize their organizational structure. Although many of the churches have come together under the Dioceses or Missions, umbrella organizations with an Archbishop at the head, they still maintain their "autonomy and manage their own affairs".

Many churches are still not affiliated to any of these umbrella organizations and operate entirely on their own. The autonomy remains an essential feature of the Faith because churches are still built by individuals under the guidance and instruction of the Holy Spirit. Therefore, many churches are buildings attached to the houses of the Leader/Mother, on lands privately owned or rented by these individuals.

With growth in membership the original structure is usually extended and improved with the assistance of members' contributions and the proceeds of fund raising ventures.

The affiliation to a Diocese ensures that the church be maintained and its administration continued in the event of the death of its founder. It also provides the avenue for the Ordination of ministers and the acquisition of the legal instrument, the marriage officers' license.

The Act of Incorporation is a legal instrument for which application can be made to the Government of the nation by any church or group of churches seeking the power to acquire property and conduct ventures to raise funds. Because incorporation can be obtained by any church applying for it, while it serves to improve the level of organization it does not serve as a measure for unification of the churches of the Faith into one body. Many dioceses, which represent groups of churches coming together under an Archbishop, have been incorporated or registered. But there are also many single churches that have become incorporated or registered.

In 1985, the National Congress of Incorporated Baptist Organizations of Trinidad and Tobago was legalized by an Act of Parliament and acknowledged as the umbrella organization for the unification and representation of Spiritual Baptists in Trinidad and Tobago. In spite of the formation of this umbrella body however, the Government still accepts applications from and passes Acts of Incorporation for individual churches and church groups, and churches are under no obligation to become members of the Congress thus rendering it inconsequential as an instrument of unification.

Notwithstanding, the fact is that the Spiritual Baptist Faith has accomplished effective growth and positive development in membership, in social standing, in media presence and involvement, in physical structures, in organization and administration and in education.

Within the Spiritual Baptist community in Trinidad and Tobago there are several incorporated bodies, among them:

1) The West Indian United Spiritual Baptist Sacred Order Incorporated.

2) The National Evangelical Spiritual Baptist Faith Archdiocese.

3) The National Ecclesiastical Council of Spiritual Baptist Churches of Trinidad and Tobago.

4) The Triune Shouters Baptist Incorporated.

5) The International Spiritual Baptist Ministerial Council of Trinidad and Tobago.

6) The Free Baptist Mission of Trinidad and Tobago.

7) The Mount Pisgah Spiritual Baptist Archdiocese International of Trinidad and Tobago

8) The Mount Garazin Shouter and Baptist Church.

9) The Mount Hope Independent Spiritual Baptist Archdiocese of Trinidad and Tobago.

10) Mount Zion Independent Spiritual Baptist Church Incorporated of Trinidad and Tobago.

11) The Little Shrine Spiritual Baptist Church.

12) The Ezekiel Spiritual Gospel Assembly.

13) The United Churches of Spiritual Baptists.

14) The Independent Spiritual Baptist Assembly.

15) Mt. Bethel National Spiritual Baptist Assembly of Trinidad and Tobago.

16) Faith International Baptist Convention of Trinidad and Tobago.

17) Divine Army of the New Creation.

18) Church of Spiritual Metaphysics.

19) Mt. Beulah Evangelical Baptist Church.

20) Council of Elders Spiritual Shouter Baptist Faith of Trinidad and Tobago.

21) Judah Spiritual Baptist Church.

22) Levitical Council of Spiritual Baptist Ministers Archdiocese.

23) Holy Faith Spiritual Baptist Tabernacle.

24) United Spiritual Baptist Association.

25) St. Peter (MCSL) Spiritual Baptist Church.

In 1981, with the approval and participation of the government but without the status of a holiday, members of the Faith began holding grand celebratory activities on March 30, in commemoration of the Repeal of the Ordinance in 1951.

In 1994, the then Government agreed to declare the day March 30, a public festival (not a holiday) commemorating the lifting of the Prohibition as recommended by a Cabinet appointed Joint Select committee.

In 1995, the incumbent Prime Minister officially opened the Southland School of Theology at Chinese Village, La Brea, on July 15, and, impressed by the achievement of the Spiritual Baptist Community, publicly promised the necessary finances and a parcel of land in the capital city of Port of Spain for a Spiritual Baptist Primary School and Cathedral. (His term ended abruptly and this promise was never fulfilled.)

In 1996, the government of the day granted to the Spiritual Baptist Faith a public holiday to be celebrated on March 30, called **Spiritual Baptist/Shouter Liberation Day** in memory of the struggle and in recognition of the **Repeal of the 1917 Prohibition Ordinance of March 30, 1951.**

In 2000, the government of the day granted lands to the three major Spiritual/Shouter Baptist organizations, now called **Baptist Boulevard in Maloney** on which stand a Spiritual/Shouter Baptist Primary School and ECCE Centre, Twelve Monumental Pillars in honour of and bearing the names of 100 Spiritual/Shouter Baptist Pioneers, erected and consecrated in 2017, at the Centenary Year Celebrations, and a thriving agricultural Reforestation Nursery Project with the National Reforestation and Watershed Rehabilitation Programme of the Ministry of Agriculture, Lands and Fisheries.

In 2016, the year from **November 2016 to November 2017, was designated the Spiritual Baptist Shouter Prohibition Ordinance Centenary Year,** in commemoration of the passing of the Shouter's Prohibition

Ordinance of November 1917, and celebration of the survival, resilience, growth and achievements of the Spiritual/Shouter Baptist community 100 years after being banned from existence. Among the many highlights of the year's activities were:

❖ the November 2016, **Media Launch** at the City Hall, Port of Spain, and **Eucharistic Service** at Mt. Zion SBC, Longdenville,

❖ the **Centenarian Celebration** of nine living Spiritual Baptist Centenarians at Chaguanas, January 2017, and **National Conference of Delegates** at JR&D's Auditorium, Princes Town,

❖ the **National Family Day and Health Fair,** Maloney, June 2017,

❖ the hosting of a **National Prison Calypso and Monologue Competition** at YTC, Golden Grove and eight **Steel and Drum Public Concerts** across the nation in July and August 2017,

❖ the theatre production of **Earl Lovelace's Wine of Astonishment** in conjunction with UTT, APA at NAPA, October 2017,

❖ the **Spiritual Baptist Shouter Freedom March** from the Waterfront, Wrightson Road to the Queen's Park Savannah, Port of Spain, November 2017.

In **2019**, the government of the day granted state lands to the Spiritual Baptist Community for Spiritual Baptist Memorial Grounds and the construction of a Spiritual Baptist Cathedral and Administrative Headquarters.

In **2020**, the government of the day fulfilled its promise to assist the Spiritual Baptist community with the construction of the Spiritual Baptist Cathedral and gifted ten million dollars $10,000,000.00 to the project, which is in progress.

CHAPTER FIVE

BELIEFS, CELEBRATIONS, AND PRACTICES OF THE SPIRITUAL BAPTIST FAITH

*Let us hold fast the profession
of our Faith without wavering,
For he is faithful that promised.
(Hebrew 10:23)*

I n spite of the differences in administration and affiliation in Spiritual Baptist churches, there are beliefs, celebrations and practices basic and common to all Spiritual Baptists who believe that Jesus Christ is Lord. The 'Beliefs' or 'Articles of Faith' as listed below are acknowledged in the *Spiritual Baptist Minister's Manual,* published by W.I.U.S.B.S.O Inc. in 1993 and widely used by Ministers throughout the Spiritual Baptist community. In *Joy Cometh In the Morning* we note that, "The Shouter Baptist also put forward the view that the tenets and practices of their religion categorized them as part of the mainstream body of Christianity". (Jacobs p. 290)

BELIEFS

1) **We** the Spiritual Baptists, believe in the *inerrancy of the Bible:* that the Holy Bible was written by men divinely inspired; that God is its author; that salvation of man is its end, and, it is the true center of Christian union.

2) **We** believe that there is only one , living and true God, infinite and holy, the Creator of heaven and earth; that there are three persons in the Trinity of the Godhead, the Father, the Son, and the Holy Spirit, equal in every divine perfection but still ONE GOD.

3) **We** believe in the virgin birth of Jesus, that He freely took upon Him our nature, yet without sin; that His death made a full atonement for our sins and is **the only and final sacrifice** for the redemption of mankind; that having arisen from the dead, He is now sitting on the throne in heaven, the only mediator between God and man.

4) **We** believe that *repentance and faith* must be wrought in man's soul by the regenerating Spirit of God; that man must be born again of water and the Spirit in holy Baptism in obedience to the Gospel; and that man must accept Jesus Christ as Prophet, Priest and King, the all Sufficient Saviour and the only begotten Son of God in order to inherit the Kingdom of God.

5) We believe that Christian Baptism is by *immersion in water of a believer,* into the name of the Father, the Son and the Holy Spirit; to show forth our faith in the crucified, buried and risen Saviour with its effect in our death to sin and resurrection to a new life; an outward sign of inward grace.

6) We believe that *God's grace* and the blessing of salvation are made free to all by the mercy of God in the Gospel and that nothing prevents the salvation of the greatest sinner on earth but his own voluntary rejection of the Gospel.

7) We believe the Scriptures teach that a visible Church of Christ is a *congregation of baptized* believers associated with covenant in the faith and fellowship of the Gospel.

8) We believe the Scriptures teach that the end of the world is approaching; that *at the last day Christ will descend from heaven* to judge the living and the dead; that the wicked will be adjudged to endless punishment and the righteous to endless joy.

9) We believe in the promise of Jesus that the Comforter, the Holy Spirit, will guide and teach believers and will speak to them through dreams and visions; that the indwelling of the Holy Spirit will manifest in the lives of believers by a holy disposition and caring attitude; and that speaking in tongues is a gift of the Holy Spirit available to

believers today as are other gifts, such as
healing and prophecy, as recorded in the Holy
Bible.

CELEBRATIONS

CHRISTMAS

This festival is celebrated to commemorate the birth of Our Lord. At *Christmas* we are brought face to face with the mystery of the incarnation, the virgin birth, the divine indwelling the human, God made man. The recounting of this great occasion fills us with joy for it marks the fulfillment of the prophecy and promise: *"Behold, a virgin shall conceive, and bear a son, and shall call his name Emmanuel". (Isaiah 7: 14)*

PASSION TIDE

Beginning with Palm Sunday the Church follows the footsteps of Jesus leading to His suffering, death and burial. *Holy Week* services provide the opportunity for the congregation to live again through the historical events of the Faith and relate them to their own lives. The week culminates in the celebration of the *Last Supper* on *Holy Thursday* night and services commemorating the death and burial on *Good Friday* when man's redemption was paid.

EASTER

The celebration of **Easter** is pervaded by the joyous realization of Christ's victory over death. Because Christ left an empty tomb the hope of eternal life and the joy of our salvation is complete. For death was swallowed up in victory. Indeed, *"If Christ be not risen, then is our preaching vain, and your faith is also vain." (1 Cor. 15: 14)*

PENTECOST

Pentecost celebrates the outpouring of the Holy Spirit, as promised by Jesus, on the disciples assembled in Jerusalem. The commemoration serves as a reminder to the Church of the importance of being in one accord and of the working and living presence of the Holy Spirit in the Church. For Spiritual Baptists the day of Pentecost is a significant event, for our life and service is underpinned by the promise of Christ that *"when he, the Spirit of truth is come, he will guide you in all truth: ... and he will shew you things to come. He shall glorify me for he shall receive of me, and shall shew it unto you." (John 16: 13-14)*

CHURCH ANNIVERSARY

The establishment of a local church embodied in the building of a house set aside specifically for the worship of God is a grand achievement. Each year, therefore, the members gather together to *reflect on the year past*, and to celebrate and give thanks to God for keeping the body of the church together in fellowship. They use the opportunity to assess their achievements, count their blessings, and dedicate the year ahead to God.

HARVEST

Harvest celebration signifies the recognition of the hand of God in the bounty of the land and of our lives, and of his mercy towards men.

THANKSGIVING

This is a festivity celebrated at various times throughout the year by members of the Faith. It is held after special occasions in their lives such as a success in undertakings and recovery from illness. It recognizes the mercy of God and expresses gratitude to God for his many blessings and his loving kindness towards man.

FLOWER AND CANDLE LIGHT SERVICE

The celebration of the *Flower Service or Candle Light Service* represents a time for stock taking. It is a time when man's life is compared to that of the flower whose beauty fades at the end of the day and the candle whose light wanes as the wax is burnt out. These symbols, the flower and the candle, are used many times in the Bible and are effective in bringing to mind the frailty of human existence. They also symbolize Jesus – *The Rose of Sharon, The Lily of the Valley, the Light of the World*, without whom we live in darkness.

OLD YEAR/NEW YEAR

Celebration of praises and thanksgiving, by keeping watch night services, acknowledges the passing of one year and the beginning of the next. The congregation gathers on Old Year's night to give God praise and thanks for the passing year and expectantly awaits New Year. They herald the New Year with rejoicing, joyous greetings and New Year resolutions.

PRACTICES

BAPTISM

We believe that repentance and faith are prerequisites for baptism, in keeping with the Biblical injunction. It is the normal practice of the Faith that candidates are given instruction over a period of time in preparation for Baptism. This preparation ends in a service of praise and rejoicing prior to the candidates' public acknowledgement of their acceptance of Jesus Christ as personal Lord and Saviour by immersion in "living water" i.e. a stream, river or sea.

INFANT DEDICATION

This service acknowledges that every child belongs to God and is the holy act of dedicating the child to God. The child is named, anointed, and offered up unto God (Luke2:22).

MOURNING/FASTING

For the Spiritual Baptist, Mourning is regarded as a unique phenomenon of the Faith in a society where several other Christian religious bodies choose a more relaxed form of worship - one without this rigidity of discipline. Mourning is characterized by the denial to one's self of the freedom to move about, to speak, to eat, drink, bathe, or any other comforts, and the acceptance of the naked earth for a bed, a stone for a pillow. Further characteristics are ceaseless praying, fasting with meditation, and feeding on the Word of God, day and night to be able to enter into spiritual travels. Mourning is considered a valuable exercise for the development of the soul, the strengthening of the Spirit, and the achieving of spiritual knowledge, wisdom and understanding. The mourner strives to bring his body, spirit and soul under the subjection of the divine will of God, with the help of the Holy Spirit.

PILGRIMAGES

These are visits from one church in one district to another church in some other district. The Leader/Mother organizes buses for the transport of his/her members as well as members from nearby churches who come to support their brethren in the endeavour. Praying and singing make the journey a joyous one. When they arrive at the destination they "meet" and "greet" their brethren "on the other side" (the other district) and are then welcomed into the Church to praise God in unity.

COMMEMORATION OF THE DEAD

Many modern day Christian Churches believe that there should be no prayer services in "commemoration of the dead." But the Spiritual Baptist Church believes, that, binding up the bruised and broken hearted is a precious ministry, since bereavement may shatter the hope of many homes and family circles. When a loved one has died, leaving behind him Godly examples of steadfastness in love towards his fellowman, and faith and obedience to the will of God, this causes an awakening to consciousness in the souls of friends and kindred and in many cases, gives birth to an urge to call upon God. It is the Minister of the Gospel who should now point the bereaved to Jesus Christ, the "Resurrection and the Life" by bringing the message of sympathy and hope, that they may realize that their greatest solace is from above.

BANDS

Bands are pieces of cloth with seals (Spiritual Writings) onthem. "Bands" are used in Baptism and Mourning for the covering of the eyes serving to "block out the carnal world" i.e. to prevent distraction by sight, and to direct and encourage concentration on things Spiritual.

DOPTION

Groaning of spiritual sounds of various rhythms while praying and during spiritual journeys, as evidenced in Paul's writing to the Romans – *"The Spirit itself maketh intercession for us with groanings which cannot be uttered." (Rom. 8:26)*

SPEAKING IN TONGUES: (TALKING UNKNOWN)

A Spiritual Gift listed in the Bible in 1 Cor. 12 as one of the gifts of the Holy Spirit, when believers speak in languages unknown to them in their normal speech. This is done on two levels among Spiritual Baptists:

    i. **As prayer or talking to God.**

    ii. **As Spiritual conversation between members who are traversing the Spiritual Realm.**

ROADSIDE PREACHING/MISSION

Members of the Faith are sent to the villages and the nation with messages received in dreams and visions. These are preached at street corners and along the streets after the manner of John the Baptist and Jesus the Christ of early Christianity.

PRAYING ALOUD

This is another practice of the Spiritual Baptist Faith in which members, individually or in groups, pray aloud during the service kneeling either at the center of the Church or at the steps of the Altar. During this time, the congregation listens or hums/sings to accompany the praying person(s).

MODE OF DRESS

Members wear uniforms/spiritual clothes in various designs and colours as received on spiritual journeys. These uniforms indicate offices and functions in the community of believers. It is imperative that women cover their heads to worship with large pieces of cloth called head-ties. Many women are recognized to be senior members of the Faith by their head-ties which are worn at all times, and not only for worship purposes.

In addition to spiritual garments received on spiritual journeys, members wear church uniforms. Ordained ministers wear ceremonial clothes received at ordination designating their rank in the hierarchy of the diocese or church.

TITLES

Offices, roles and functions in the Faith are identified by titles such as Leader, Mother, Teacher, Pointer, Baptizer, Shepherd, Nurse, Prover, Watchman, Captain, Surveyor and Healer.

LEADER is the title given to the head of the "home" i.e. the church. He is the officiating minister and is gifted in controlling/leading the flock/membership. In these modern days the leader is often an ordained minister called Reverend. He may also have other spiritual designations e.g. Pointer, Teacher.

MOTHER is the female counterpart of the leader, the female head of the home. It is also a spiritual designation of one who cares for other members in the church and one who has spiritual children.

TEACHER is the title of one (male or female) who has attained spiritual heights sufficient to instruct, 'teach' other members in the Faith. The Teacher is also often, but not always a leader/mother or pointer as well.

POINTER is the person (male or female) who "seals bands" and places the mourner on the mourning ground. The Pointer therefore "points" the way for the pilgrim (mourner) and is responsible for the welfare of the pilgrim during mourning. This is one of the gifts of the Spirit gained during mourning and its administration is dependent on Spiritual instructions.

BAPTISER is the person (male) who has the spiritual authority to perform the act of baptism and administer the vow of allegiance to Jesus Christ for the candidates who have been prepared at the church for the journey to River Jordan (the river or sea) where the ceremony is conducted.

SURVEYOR is the one (male) who surveys the pool (water) for Baptism. He chooses a portion of the water (river or sea) setting boundaries to it for the purpose of performing the baptismal rites. The Baptiser is also a Surveyor.

SHEPHERD is a spiritual leader with responsibility for guiding and caring for the flock (membership). It is a spiritual gift usually received early in one's spiritual career by those who are potential leaders. The female counterpart is the SHEPHERDESS.

NURSE is the name given to the member (usually female) who attends to the needs of candidates and pilgrims during the rites of Baptism and Mourning. This title also represents a Spiritual Gift.

PROVER is the spiritual office of one (usually male) whose duty it is to prove whether the spiritual activity in progress is of truth and/or if the claims of a pilgrim or member are authentic. He is a discerner of spirit and spiritual manifestation.

WATCHMAN (usually male) is one who stands guard (sometimes at the door) and is alert to the arrival of visitors and their activities and intentions. In olden days the Watchman often warned the camp of the approach of the police and this foiled many "raids". Most Provers are also Watchmen but Watchmen are not necessarily Provers.

CAPTAIN as the name suggests is one (male) in charge of, or responsible for, the ship (the church while service is in progress). It is a senior office. The Captain is second to the Leader and is often a Leader. His duty is to ensure that the ship sails smoothly and well i.e. that the service is carried out with vigour and vitality in the spirit of holiness and pure worship.

HEALER is any member (male or female) gifted with the art of healing the sick. This may be done by praying with the sick or by prescribing medicines or administering treatment.

SOME ICONS OR SYMBOLIC SACRED ITEMS USED IN THE FAITH

SHEPHERD ROD AND STAFF – symbolic of the divine authority and virtue of the office of shepherd – Jesus, the Good Shepherd.

BELL – symbolic of "the voice of one crying in the wilderness" to call sinners to repentance; used to signify the beginning (the call to worship) and the ending of the service or in response to the sound of spiritual bells or according to spiritual instructions. The High Priest wore bells to signify, by their ringing when he moved, that he was still alive. Jesus our High Priest is still alive.

TARIA AND LOTHAR – vessels used in the church. The **Lothar**, symbolic of the holy state of man before God in worship, contains water and flowers. The flowers beautify the church and symbolize peace, love and joy kept alive by the water of life. The **Taria** symbolizes the circle of divinity within which man places himself in worship before God. In it stands the lothar amid **grains** which are symbolic of the grace of God.

GLASS – with water – symbolic of the pure river of water proceeding from the throne of God is also a receptacle for flowers or bushes representing the tree of life in the midst of that river.

CALABASH – the first and original vessel made by God's own hands also contains water and flowers to beautify the Church.

CANDLES AND CANDLESTICK – The candlestick is symbolic of the Church and the candles, the spirit of the Church. The candlestick serves to hold the candles which provide light and are symbolic of the light of the world – Jesus.

INCENSE – provides a sweet smelling savour signifying the prayer of faith. The rising of the smoke represents the rising of the prayers of the faithful to the Godhead.

FLOWERS – God's handiwork, used to decorate the Altar, Centre pole and Corners of the Church, representing man's first habitation, the Garden of Eden and signifying the beauty as well as the frailty and brevity of life.

WATER – used for washing, cleansing, consecrating and drinking – these uses are physical and practical as well as symbolic and spiritual.

OIL – used for anointing, as recorded in the Bible for healing and blessing. Anointing is of great spiritual significance and is used to make things hallowed.

CENTRE POLE – is the central point of the Church – symbolic of Jesus, the central point of worship, where the prayers of the membership are offered. The physical pole (which is not generally present in churches today) is also symbolic of the connection between earth and heaven; a connection which is maintained by prayer.

ALTAR – The highest level in the church is the symbol of believing and acceptable prayer, the place for the priest's sacrifice of praise and worship. It is the place of the *mercy seat* where God promised to meet with his servants and answer prayer and is present in the heavenly Temple as described in Revelation Chapter 8. The Altar is adorned with vessels and flowers, candlesticks, and candles.

BIBLE – the written Word of God, the Scriptures of Christianity, the Chart and Compass of the Spiritual Baptist Faith. God is its author; the salvation of man is its end. Readings and lessons from the Bible form the matter of the sermons preached and lessons taught in the Spiritual Baptist Church. The Bible is often called the Sword.

CROSS – the intersection of God's love and justice, the centrepoint of His plan of redemption for mankind. It is the symbol of *Sacrifice* and the emblem of *Victory*. The Cross symbolises, for the believer, Salvation from sin.

APPENDIX

CORRECTING POPULAR INACCURATE THEORIES OF ORIGIN

Then said He,
Lo I come to do thy will, O God.
He taketh away the first,
that he may establish the second.
By the which will we are sanctified
through the offering of the body of Jesus
Christ once for all.
(Hebrews 10:9-10)

1. ERROR

"several published sources credit an Englishman, George Cowen, with establishing the first Baptist missionary outpost on the island of Trinidad in 1843." (Stapleton, P. 8)

CORRECTION
From the data in Chapter One we recognize that Cowen

did not begin the Baptist Movement instead the Baptist Missionary Society occasioned a split among the Baptists already here and the attachment of names to the resulting groups, viz... London, Independent and Spiritual Baptists.

2. ERROR

"The Shouters... seem ... to have flourished exceedingly in St. Vincent and to have made themselves an unmitigated nuisance that they had to be legislated out of existence. Then they came to Trinidad." (Attorney General, Hon. H. Cowper-Golian, K.C. 1917).

CORRECTION

The history of Trinidad shows that Baptists were "shouting" more than half a century before 1912 when the Vincentian Shakers had to flee persecution in their island. History also shows that Africans were brought to Trinidad from the other islands as early as the eighteenth century; St. Vincent was not excluded from the list. So that the influence is not denied, but the idea of mass movement leading to origin is grossly incorrect.

3. ERROR

The Spiritual Baptist Faith originated in Africa and was brought here by the slaves and "can safely be said to be an off shoot from the Orisha cult." (Gopaul, p. vii)

CORRECTION

The Africans came from various tribes and regions of Africa and were kept separated to avoid the possibility of insurrection. Whatever practices were carried out had to emerge from a coalition of the varied memories and practices. Further, the "Orisha Cult" is representative of the religious practices of one region and one tribe and cannot therefore have been the source or root of all African beliefs. Africa had by this time been acquainted with various expressions of the African Traditional Religions as well as Islam and Christianity. Orisha is the reinterpretation of African Traditional Religion. Spiritual Baptist is the reinterpretation of Christianity.

4. ERROR

Arising out of the third theory is this fourth which claims that Spiritual Baptist and Orisha (Shango) are the same.

CORRECTION

This is easily refuted because Baptists are Christians, the early Spiritual Baptist/Shouters were spreading the message of Jesus Christ. The

Orisha (Shango) devotees do not accept Jesus Christ as *Son of God and Saviour of the souls of men.* The Spiritual Baptist Faith is the Faith of Africans in Trinidad worshipping Jesus as Lord and Master of the world. **Because they are two different belief systems they are two different religions.** The members of both have the same history and culture in common, but not the same religion.

5. ERROR

The Spiritual Baptist Faith is an African religion only for people of African descent

CORRECTION

Jesus Christ died for all men. Bethlehem is not in Europe, neither is Jordan in North/South America, nor is Jerusalem in England. Christianity began among the Jews but all Jews are not Christians and all Christians are not Jews. The Spiritual Baptist Faith is the continuation of the Apostolic Tradition of Christianity emerging among Africans in Trinidad and open to all who believe that Jesus Christ is Lord and desire to serve Him in Spirit and in Truth.

10.1.18

TRINIDAD and TOBAGO.

No. 27—1917.

I ASSENT,

[L.S.]

J. R. CHANCELLOR,
Governor.

28th November, 1917.

AN ORDINANCE to render illegal indulgence in the practices of the body known as the Shouters.

[*28th November, 1917.*]

BE it enacted by the Governor of Trinidad and Tobago with the advice and consent of the Legislative Council thereof as follows:—

1. This Ordinance may be cited as the Shouters' Pro- Short Title. hibition Ordinance, 1917.

2.—(1.) A "Shouters' meeting" means a meeting or Definition of gathering of two or more persons, whether indoors or in the "Shouters' meeting." open air, at which the customs and practices of the body known as Shouters (hereafter in this Ordinance referred to as "the Shouters") are indulged in. The decision of any Magistrate in any case brought under this Ordinance as to whether the customs and practices are those of the Shouters shall be final, whether the persons indulging in

3

No. 27.   "*Shouters.*"   1917.

6. It shall be an offence against this Ordinance for any
person at or in the vicinity of any Shouters' meeting to
commit or cause to be committed or to induce or to
persuade to be committed any act of indecency.

Acts of indecency or immorality.

7.—(1.) It shall be lawful for any party of members of
the Constabulary Force, of whom one shall be a commissioned or non-commissioned officer, without a warrant
to enter at any time of the day or night any house, estate,
land or place in or on which such commissioned or non-
commissioned officer may have good ground to believe or
suspect that a Shouters' meeting is being held or where he
may have good ground to believe or suspect that any person
or persons is or are being kept for the purpose of initiation
into the ceremonies of the Shouters' and to take the names
and addresses of all persons present at such Shouters' meeting or Shouters' house.

Police may enter without warrant house or place where Shouters' meeting is being held.

(2.) It shall also be lawful for any member of the Constabulary Force to demand the names and addresses of any
persons taking part in any meeting in the open air which
he has good reason to believe is a Shouters' meeting.

(3.) Any person refusing to give his name and address
to any member of the Constabulary Force when asked to
do so under the authority of this section shall be liable to
be arrested and to be detained at a Constabulary station
until his identity can be established.

8. Any person guilty of an offence against this Ordinance
shall be liable on summary conviction before a Magistrate
to a fine not exceeding £50 and in default of payment
thereof to imprisonment with or without hard labour for a
term not exceeding six months.

Penalties

Passed in Council this Sixteenth day of November,
in the year of Our Lord one thousand nine hundred and
seventeen.

HARRY L. KNAGGS,
Clerk of the Council.

Teacher Hazel De Peza

TRINIDAD and TOBAGO

No. 20—1951

[L.S.]

I ASSENT,

H. E. RANCE,
Governor.
12th April, 1951.

AN ORDINANCE to remove the prohibition hitherto placed upon the Practices of the Body known as the Shouters.

Commencement

[*26th April,* 1951.]

Enactment

ENACTED by the Governor of Trinidad and Tobago with the advice and consent of the Legislative Council thereof.

Short title

1. This Ordinance may be cited as the Shouters Prohibition (Repeal) Ordinance, 1951.

2. The Shouters Prohibition Ordinance is hereby repealed. _{Repeal of Ch. 4. No. 19}

Passed in Council this thirtieth day of March, in the year of Our Lord one thousand nine hundred and fifty-one.

W. FUNG,
Clerk of the Council.

1951

TRINIDAD AND TOBAGO
PRINTED AND PUBLISHED BY THE GOVERNMENT PRINTER

POSTSCRIPT

To the Readers and Teachers

"We have many things we can use as our springboard to glory. It is what a man has which should be the source of his glory. We must not use our own hands to relegate our own culture to a backward position" advises the Oni of lfe Sijuwade, Oba Kunade, Olubase II.

The time has come to arrest the misconceptions perpetuated by scholars and laymen who study the Faith from the outside and know not of what they speak. "For I know whom I have believed." **(2 Tim. 1:12)**

The Spiritual Baptist Faith must be recognized for what it is: **the only indigenous Christian grouping in Trinidad and Tobago.** "Base things of the world, and things which are despised, hath God chosen yea." (1 Cor. 1: 28)

Spiritual Baptists are members of that body of Christians who in their mode of worship show forth the prophecies of Joel:

"And in the last days, saith God, I will pour out my Spirit upon all flesh; and your sons and your daughters shall prophesy, and your young men shall see visions and your old men shall dream dreams." (Acts 2:17)

BIBLIOGRAPHY

BARRETT, Leonard E. – Soul Force - African Heritage in Afro-American Religion, Anchor Press, New York, 1974.

CARROLL, J. M. – The Trail of Blood, Ashland Avenue, Baptist Church, Kentucky, 1931.

GIBBS DE PEZA, Hazel Ann – Correcting Misconceptions: A Review of Caribbean Studies Theses on the Topic - The Spiritual Baptist Faith, B.A. Thesis, The University of the West Indies, St. Augustine, Trinidad, 1989. (E-book, Trafford Publishing, 2012)

 – Glossolalia in the Spiritual Baptist Faith - A Linguistic Study, Dissertation, The University of the West Indies, St. Augustine, Trinidad. (Unpublished) 1996 (a).

GIBBS DE PEZA, H.A. Rev. (Editor) – Call Him by His Name – Jesus. Fishnet Publications, CEPAC – Network, Trinidad, 1996 (b).

GOPAUL - WHITTINGTON, V. – History and Writings of the Spiritual Baptists, Printing Plus, St. James, Trinidad. n.d.

82

HACKSHAW, John M. – The Baptist Denomination, A&B Jackson Memorial Society, Trinidad & Tobago, 1992.

JACOBS, Curtis M. – Joy Comes In The Morning. Caribbean Historical Society, Trinidad, 1996.

RICHARDSON, F. Rev. – The Origin Of The Baptists n.p., Trinidad, n.d.

SOUTHLAND SCHOOL OF THEOLOGY – The Spiritual Baptist Minister's Manual, The WIUSBSO Inc., Trinidad, 1993

STAPLETON, A.L. Archbishop – The Birth And Growth Of The Spiritual Baptist Faith (commonly called Shouters). Sooklal Printery, Siparia, Trinidad, 1983.

THOMAS, Eudora – Short History Of The Spiritual Baptists (commonly called Shouters), Community Development Press, Trinidad, n.d.

WARNER-LEWIS, M. – Guinea's Other Suns, Majority Press, U.S.A. 1991.

WILLIAMS, Eric E. – History Of The People Of Trinidad and Tobago Andre Deutsch, London, 1964.

YOUNG, J.U. – Black And African Theologies: Siblings or Distant Cousins? Orbis Books, New York, 1983.

REVIEW

This book is a vivid and engrossing account of the history, struggle and growth of the Spiritual Baptist Church in Trinidad. It is a book produced in order to bring to the current discourse on this often misunderstood and maligned religious community some rational and research-based information in order to counter long held misconceptions about the nature of the sect.

The Spiritual Baptist Faith is the name given to the Christian religious group emerging among the Africans in the 19th Century in Trinidad. In 1917, the group was called the Shouters because of their expressive worship practices and an Ordinance was passed against their mode of worship which was considered to be "too noisy, too African and therefore uncivilized and unacceptable" in a western oriented multi-racial colony.

Since those early years of struggle for survival, the story of the Baptist Church in Trinidad has been akin to that of the ancient Israelites in their efforts to establish themselves in Canaan amidst hostile neighbours. The road for the Baptist has been long and hard and a modest victory was achieved in 1951 when the Legislative Council repealed the Ordinance which had virtually criminalized the sect. In 1996, the Government of Trinidad and Tobago agreed to declare March 30, a public holiday called Spiritual Baptist/ Shouter Liberation Day.

This is an authenticated account of the history, beliefs, practices and policies of this highly visible and still controversial sect and Hazel Ann Gibbs DePeza brings sensitivity, profound faith and balance to the story of this community which has traditionally been marginalized in law and custom. This book reveals the essential tenets of the Spiritual Baptist Faith and is a highly convincing piece of scholarly writing. It is written in a clear and concise manner, outlining the key doctrines and explaining terminology to the reader. It is a timely and distinctly welcome study on one of Trinidad's most vibrant religious sects.

Ival Melville Myers Ed.D.
Curriculum Officer,
Social Studies/ History.

www.ingramcontent.com/pod-product-compliance
Lightning Source LLC
Chambersburg PA
CBHW031220120626
46545CB00003B/924

* 9 7 8 1 9 5 8 1 7 6 5 6 6 *